AUG -- 2017

Ronald Reagan

BY KATY S. DUFFIELD

Published by The Child's World®
1980 Lookout Drive • Mankato, MN 56003-1705
800-599-READ • www.childsworld.com

Acknowledgments
The Child's World®: Mary Swensen, Publishing Director
Red Line Editorial: Editorial direction and production
The Design Lab: Design

Photographs ©: Bettmann/Corbis, cover, 1; AS400 DB/
Corbis, 4, 11; Underwood & Underwood/Corbis, 7; Snap/Rex/
Newscom, 8; Glasshouse Images/Newscom, 12; AP Images,
15; Wally McNamee/Corbis, 16; Peter Turnley/Corbis, 19; Ron
Edmonds/AP Images, 21

ISBN 9781503808744
LCCN 2015958440

Printed in the United States of America
Mankato, MN
June, 2016
PA02303

ABOUT THE AUTHOR

Katy S. Duffield has a BA in English
from the University of Illinois–
Springfield. She is the author of more
than 20 books for children and has
written both fiction and nonfiction for
many children's magazines.

Table of Contents

Ronald "Dutch" Reagan worked as a
lifeguard for seven summers.

CHAPTER ONE

Hardworking Hero

Night was falling on the Rock River in Dixon, Illinois. Seventeen-year-old Dutch Reagan pulled a whistle from around his neck. It had been a long, hot day. Dutch was ready to go home.

Just then, a cry rang out. Water splashed into the air. A man struggled in the river. He tried to keep his head above water.

Dutch knew what to do. He dove into the fast-moving water. He swam toward the man. Just in time, Dutch pulled him to safety.

Dutch made sure the man was okay. Then Dutch walked over to an old log. He pulled out his pocketknife. He carved a notch into the wood.

Lots of marks stretched down the log. This was not the first life Dutch had saved. The marks counted all the people Dutch had helped in Rock River.

In all, Dutch saved 77 swimmers as a lifeguard. Being a lifeguard was hard work. But Dutch didn't mind. He cared about people. He liked helping them.

Dutch worked hard for most of his life. He took time to help people. He also took time to listen to what they had to say.

These qualities helped Dutch become a great man. Eventually, they helped him become the president of the United States.

Reagan went to high school in the 1920s.

Ronald Reagan as a young boy with his father, John, his older brother, Neil, and his mother, Nellie

CHAPTER TWO

A Young Dutch Reagan

★ ★ ★

It was February 6, 1911. A baby was born in Illinois. The baby's father took a close look him. He said, "He looks like a fat little Dutchman!" The baby's parents named him Ronald Wilson Reagan. But for many years he would be called "Dutch."

As a boy, Dutch liked to ice skate. He liked to read and swim. He also liked art. Dutch thought he might grow up to be a firefighter or an artist.

In high school, one of Dutch's favorite activities was football. Dutch wasn't very big. But he worked hard. He refused to give up. He finally earned his way onto the starting team. Dutch found another passion, too: acting. He began to perform in school plays.

Dutch graduated from high school in 1928. He hoped to go to college. But he didn't have much money. Dutch's football talents helped though. He got a football **scholarship**. The scholarship paid for part of his fees. He washed dishes and worked at other jobs to cover the rest.

In 1932, Dutch graduated from college. He needed a job. But Dutch longed to go to Hollywood. He wanted to star in movies. However, Dutch didn't think he could make a living as an actor.

So Dutch got a different job. He worked for a radio station. He became a **sportscaster**. Dutch

Reagan worked as a radio announcer for WOC Radio in Davenport, Iowa.

talked about football and baseball games. He told what was happening at track meets.

Dutch enjoyed life as a sportscaster. But in his heart, he still wanted to be an actor.

Reagan on the set of his ninth movie, *Girls on Probation*

CHAPTER THREE

Lights! Camera! Action!—Governor!

★ ★ ★

In the spring of 1937, Dutch had a chance to make his dreams come true. He went to Hollywood, California. If he wanted to act, Hollywood was the place to be.

A friend helped Dutch get a **screen test**. He got a **script**. Over and over, Dutch practiced his lines. Then, he went in front of a camera. He performed his lines for Warner Brothers film studios.

Warner Brothers liked what they saw. But they did not like the name "Dutch." So they decided to use his real name instead.

Ronald Reagan made his first movie in 1937. It was called *Love Is on the Air.* That was only the beginning. Reagan became a popular movie star. Over time, he appeared in more than 50 movies.

In 1954, Reagan got a new job. He became the host of a TV show. It was called *The General Electric Theater.* Even more people got to know Reagan. As part of his job, he traveled. He made speeches. He talked about making movies. Later, he began talking about **politics**.

People liked Reagan. They thought he was a strong speaker. They thought he had good ideas. They believed he could make California a better place to live. Some California business people asked Reagan

Reagan was elected governor of California with the majority of votes on November 6, 1966.

to run for governor. In 1966, Reagan ran for the office. And he won.

Running the state was a hard job. California had problems. The state was in debt. This means the state owed money that it didn't have. Reagan helped balance the budget. He helped get California back on track.

Reagan served two **terms** as governor. He was ready to take a break. But Reagan had become a popular man. People didn't want him to leave politics. His success as governor led him to be the top choice for president.

Reagan was elected president in 1980.

CHAPTER FOUR

The President of the United States

In 1976, Reagan ran for president. He didn't win. But he came close. Reagan ran again in 1980. This time, he won. He became the 40th president of the United States.

In 1980, America had some problems. **Taxes** were high. Many people did not have jobs. They were not proud of their country. Reagan hoped to change that.

Reagan felt the government had too much control. He wanted people to believe in America again.

Reagan started to work. He put his ideas into place. Then, something horrible happened. On March 30, 1981, Reagan was shot. He had given a speech in Washington, DC. When he walked outside, a man shot him. The man was John Hinckley Jr. Reagan was rushed to the hospital. He was hurt badly. But he survived. Hinckley was arrested for the crime.

Reagan could not wait to get back to work. He even had a few meetings in his pajamas. Reagan worked to create jobs. He lowered taxes. He made it easier to work with the government.

Reagan had done a lot for his country. But he hoped to do more. Reagan got that chance. In 1984, he was reelected.

Reagan worked to make the United States safer. He met with an important leader from the Soviet

Reagan met with Mikhail Gorbachev at the 1987 White House Summit.

Union. His name was Mikhail Gorbachev. The two men signed a **treaty**. It decreased the number of **weapons** the two countries could have. It was an important step. It made the world more secure.

Reagan also faced struggles as a president. He became involved in a **scandal**. Weapons were sold to Iran. The sale was done in secret. And it was against the law. Some people lost their jobs. But Reagan remained in office.

Soon, it was Reagan's last day as president. He left office in January 1989. He said, "It's been the honor of my life to be your president."

Reagan continued to travel. He still made speeches. He also spent time at his ranch in California. Reagan liked being outdoors. He liked riding his horses.

In 1994, Reagan wrote a letter. He told Americans that he was sick. He had a brain illness called Alzheimer's. It would make him forget the things that happened in his life.

Reagan giving his Farewell Address to the nation on his last day of office.

After that, Reagan stayed close to home. He became sicker and weaker. Ronald Reagan died on June 5, 2004. He was 93 years old. Reagan helped ease tensions with the Soviet Union. He also helped many people get jobs. He was an admired president and leader.

1900

←— **February 6, 1911** Reagan is born in Tampico, Illinois.

←— **1928** Reagan graduates from Dixon High School in Illinois.

←— **1932** Reagan graduates from Eureka College in Illinois.
           He becomes a sportscaster.

←— **1937** Reagan appears in his first movie.

←— **1954** Reagan begins hosting the TV show *GE Theater*.

←— **November 8, 1966** Reagan is elected governor of California.

←— **November 4, 1980** Reagan is elected president of the
           United States.

←— **March 30, 1981** Reagan is shot in front of a Washington, DC hotel.

←— **November 4, 1984** Reagan is reelected president.

←— **December 8, 1987** Reagan and the Soviet Union sign a treaty.

←— **November 5, 1994** Reagan announces his illness.

←— **June 5, 2004** Reagan dies in California.

2010

politics (PAWL-ih-tiks) Politics are activities to gain or hold onto power in government. Reagan became interested in politics when he was an actor.

scandal (SCAN-dahl) A scandal is something that is shocking and wrong. Reagan went through a scandal during his presidency.

scholarship (SCAH-lor-ship) A scholarship is money that a school or organization gives to help students pay for college. Reagan got a scholarship from Eureka College.

screen test (SKREEN TEST) A screen test shows if a person should be given a part in a movie. Reagan said his lines in front of a camera for his screen test.

script (SKRIPT) A script is the lines of a movie or play that are written on paper. Reagan studied a script when he was in a movie.

sportscaster (SPORTS-cass-ter) A sportscaster is a person who describes the actions of a sports event. Reagan's first job after college was as a sportscaster.

taxes (TAKS-is) Taxes are money that people and companies pay to the government. Reagan had to raise taxes when he was the governor of California.

terms (TERMS) Terms are periods of time an official serves in office. Reagan served two terms as president.

treaty (TREE-tee) A treaty is an official agreement made by two or more countries. Reagan made a treaty with the Soviet Union.

weapons (WEH-punz) Weapons are something that are used when fighting. The secret sale of weapons was a problem when Reagan was president.

In the Library

Allen, Susan and Leslie Harrington. *The Remarkable Ronald Reagan: Cowboy and Commander in Chief*. Washington, DC: Regnery Kids, 2013.

Amoroso, Cynthia. *Ronald Reagan*. Mankato, MN: Child's World, 2009.

Benge, Janet and Geoff Benge. *Ronald Reagan: Destiny at His Side*. Washington, DC: Emerald Books, 2011.

On the Web

Visit our Web site for links about Ronald Reagan: **childsworld.com/links**

Note to Parents, Teachers, and Librarians: We routinely verify our Web links to make sure they are safe and active sites. So encourage your readers to check them out!

INDEX